TABLE OF CONTENTS

Unless otherwise indicated, all Scripture quotations are taken from the King James Version of the Bible.
7 Rituals of Honor that Guarantee The Favor of God · ISBN 1-56394-402-2/B-285
Copyright © 2008 by *MIKE MURDOCK*
All publishing rights belong exclusively to Wisdom International
Publisher/Editor: Deborah Murdock Johnson
Published by The Wisdom Center · 4051 Denton Highway · Fort Worth, Texas 76117
1-817-759-BOOK · 1-817-759-0300
You Will Love Our Website...! www.WisdomOnline.com

Accuracy Department: To our Friends and Partners...We welcome any comments on errors or misprints you find in our book...Email our department: AccuracyDept@thewisdomcenter.tv. Your aid in helping us excel is highly valued.

If You Succeed...It Will Be
Because Of Someone
You Chose To Honor.
   If You Fail...It Will Be
Because Of Someone
   You Chose To Dishonor.

-MIKE MURDOCK

WHY I WROTE THIS BOOK

Honor Is The Rewarding Of Difference.
It is when you recognize and celebrate the distinctions of another. That is why developing daily Rituals of Honor are valuable in your Christian life.

Habits And Rituals Of Honor

Remember: Habit Will Take You Further Than Passion. If you fail, it will be because of a habit. If you succeed, it will be because of a habit.

I learned this through Mary Kay Ash. She understood Success Habits. Her first habit of every day was Planning The Day. She wrote down six things on a sheet of paper that she wanted to do...in the order of their importance. She did it every day of her life from 1963. When she died, her worth was $300 million. On Wall Street, her business, Mary Kay Cosmetics, was worth $1.2 billion. *Planning a day was her way of honoring her day.*

Daniel prayed three times a day.

David prayed seven times a day.

Great men are men of Ritual. Rituals decide the rhythm of life. Rituals decide your future. Rituals carry you...when disappointment weighs you down. When feelings fail you, your Rituals will not. There is no power on earth like habit and ritual.

A dear friend of mine runs five miles every day. I asked him one day, "Pete, how do you have the energy? How do you keep yourself excited?"

"I don't think about it," he explained. "I've done it for so many years, it's my habit. Every day that's what I do. Rain, sleet or snow, I run five miles a day." *I don't even think about it.* Discipline becomes habit. Habit is easy. Ritual becomes instinctive.

Habit is a gift from God. We think of bad habits, but a habit means anything you do twice gets easier. A habit is something you do instinctively without effort. What starts as discipline becomes a habit.

Note the difference between Discipline and Habits. Self-discipline is concentrated constraint, effort and focus to perform something that is unnatural and not instinctive. Its purpose is to birth a *Habit.* Habit is something you do instinctively, without forethought and the severity of conscious effort. Discipline requires constant effort, constant attention, and that is not necessarily a happy lifestyle. It is usually for a limited time...to birth the habit, a routine or action that eventually becomes natural. Studies reveal that it takes 21 consecutive days of Discipline to birth a new Habit. Incidentally, if you miss a day, you must begin your 21 days over again!

Habit is a wonderful and glorious gift from God. It simply means that anything you do twice becomes easier. It is a tool that helps you form a Life Track to run on daily.

Ritual and ceremony...are important parts of establishing what is important, what is worthy of attention and stabilizing our lives. God uses Ceremony differently than He uses Creativity. Creativity is different than Rituals. God is also a God of Habit, Custom and Rituals.

Creativity births a *Change.*

Habits birth a *Future.*

There is a need for relaxation, rest, change and creativity. There is also a great need for Daily Rituals in our life...that nurture focus, comfort zones and makes rhythm easy for a day to flow.

Rituals sustain us, comfort us and stabilize us.

Rituals of Honor decide every success you will experience with God and man. Unless you learn this, every fresh effort to succeed will be another experience in futility and failure.

Habit Will Take You Further Than Desire. When Desire runs out, Habit keeps on going. When your passion runs low, The Rituals will keep you on track.

Rituals of Honor will guarantee the Divine Favor of God.

That's why I wrote this book.

Mike Murdock

Our Prayer Together...

"Father, thank You today for Your Presence.

Thank You for Your Word. We are in love with You, Jesus. There is no one like You. We know that You are alive because You are alive *inside* of us. *The proof that You arose again is in the Changes Your Presence created in us.*

Your *Power* has changed our weakness into *strength.* Your *Presence* has changed our nature to hate into a supernatural love. We *love* Your Presence. Your Presence *within us* is the *proof* that You are truly, truly alive.

Your Favor matters more than anything on earth. Teach us how to honor You...every single day of our life. In Jesus' Name, Amen."

Your Reaction To
    The Word Of God Is
A Picture Of Your Respect
    For God.

-MIKE MURDOCK

1

THE RITUAL OF READING THE BIBLE

The Word Of God Is The Wisdom Of God.

Your Reaction To The Word Of God Is Your Reaction To God Himself. Review Deuteronomy 6:1: "Now these are the commandments the statutes, and the judgments, which the Lord your God commanded to teach you."

Remember that even the Fear of God is *taught*. Your Mentorship has decided your persuasions. Human experiences vary. No experience is similar nor can be guaranteed. Only one man, Moses, had a burning bush experience in Scripture.

That is why we teach *Rituals of Honor*. Even children must be taught the Ritual of Honor toward parents. An example is teaching them to respond respectfully with "Yes, sir" or "No, sir" instead of a dismissive "Yeah..."

Rituals of Honor are the foundation of all military organizations, the Army, Air Force, Marines and Navy. Saluting a superior officer is a Ritual of Honor.

Rituals of Honor occur every hour of the day in our culture. That is why we shake hands, bow, or embrace each other when we meet or greet.

Rituals of Honor control the quality and longevity of every marriage. Even if it is the simple ceremony of opening the car door for your wife, it is a Ritual of Honor.

There are Rituals of Honor that are very powerful in the Kingdom lifestyle.

Honor is the recognition and celebration of another's distinction.

Read Deuteronomy, chapter 6 verses 1 and 2: "Now these are the commandments, the statutes, and the judgments, which the Lord your God commanded to teach you, that ye might do them in the land whither ye go to possess it: That thou mightest fear the Lord thy God, to keep all His statutes and His commandments, which I command thee, thou, and thy son, and thy son's son."

Generational Thinking

The difference between poverty and wealth is Generational Thinking. Impoverished people do not think generationally. Their focus is daily survival. But if you converse with the ultra wealthy, their emphasis is the planning ahead of their investments, their children and grandchildren. Top Japanese companies are now thinking 300 years in advance. (Twenty years ago they planned 100 years in advance).

Wisdom is simply thinking ahead. The difference in Wisdom is in how far ahead you are willing to think. Think multi-generationally. This is why The Wealthy leave wills. The Poor rarely leave wills. Consequently, their children cannot experience accumulation. So, the government usually ends up taking everything the average man has accumulated at his death.

The average man does not have a will because he is *not* thinking ahead. He is not thinking generationally. When you start thinking generationally, your decisions are better, they last longer, they produce instant fruit.

Most of us are thinking, "What am I going to do today?" We should be thinking, "If I keep doing what I am doing, where will I be within 5 years?"

Sam Walton, who left each of his five children $1 billion, taught a very strong and very powerful concept on thinking ahead. He would never invest in a company unless he could anticipate their success 10 to 20 years in advance. He taught to never invest in a company based on the way it is today. Look at the character of the Board, the man who started it and look at the eventual need in the market for that specific product.

I remember what stirred me to birth our website. I read the comment of a wealthy man, "If your company can succeed today without a website, you will be out of business within 5 years." I believed it because of his history of wise decisions. It has made a profound difference in our ministry.

Your website gives information without the draining of your energy. Information without the expense of your time, your energy and your money. And energy is more important than money. Money is replaceable. Energy is not.

Today is your Seed for your Future. Today is the proof that you have survived your past. Recognizing that Divine Harvest births gratitude and thankfulness. *The Thankful Are Always The Happy.* God gave you today as a Seed, an Investment. Today is a Seed for any

Future...*that you want. The Quality Of Today Will Determine The Quality Of Your Future.*

That is why I am very attentive and passionate about Moments. *Every Moment.*

Each Moment is your Seed for the Minute.

Each Minute is your Seed for the Hour.

Each Hour is your Seed for Today.

Today is your Seed for the Future.

Read this in Deuteronomy 6:2-3: "That thou mightest fear the Lord thy God, to keep all His statutes and His commandments, which I command thee, thou, and thy son, and thy son's son, all the days of thy life; and that thy days may be prolonged. Hear therefore, O Israel, and observe to do it; that it may be well with thee, and that ye may increase mightily."

Something You Are Doing Is Deciding Your Financial Health. Your Increase, Favor and Joy.

God does not decide the quality of your life.

Your *Decisions* Decide The Quality Of Your Life. The government does not decide the quality of my life. It is popular to blame "government" for everything. There is no quicker way to escape the responsibility of your personal decision. Remember the 331 references in the Bible to your Decision-Making...such as Isaiah 1:19, "...If ye be willing and obedient, ye shall eat [reap] the good of the land." The Bible has 800,000 words in it. It takes 56 hours to read it through. So, the blessings of God are not even decided by God! They are decided by your own behavior, your daily conduct. Something you are *doing,* something you are *saying* is determining a Divine Reaction to you.

Your Behavior Determines Divine Favor.

"...that it may be well with thee, and that ye may

increase mightily," (Deuteronomy 6:3). Increase...is always in the mind of God for you.

Obedience is the Seed for *Intimacy.*

Intimacy is the Seed for *Learning.*

Learning is the Seed for *Increase.* Everything God touches...*multiplies.* Remember the loaves and fishes that Jesus multiplied to feed the crowd?

God kills anything that refuses to grow. Remember the man with one talent? Remember the fig tree that bore no fruit? Your unchanging need to experience, accumulate and increase is not something you can overcome. It is the Divine nature of God at work within you...the passion to become everything God wants you to be. There is a reason you want an extra car. There is a reason you want another tie. There is a reason you want an investment rental house after you buy your own house. Something is unnatural with someone who does not want to increase. This passion for multiplication is a Divine Instinct.

Increase is in your DNA.

Increase is the *fruit* of the God-life.

God has always used the Promise of Increase as His incentive to motivate you toward Obedience.

The Ritual Of Daily Teaching

Deuteronomy 6:5-9: "And thou shalt love the Lord thy God with all thine heart, and with all thy soul, and with all thy might. And these words, which I command thee this day, shall be in thine heart: And thou shalt teach them *diligently* unto thy children, and shalt talk of them when thou *sittest* in thine house, and when thou *walkest* by the way, and when thou *liest* down, and when thou *risest* up. And thou shalt bind them for a sign *upon thine hand,* and they shall be as frontlets *between thine eyes.* And thou shalt write them *upon the posts of thy house, and on thy gates."*

The first Divine Ritual commanded is to study and teach The Word of God...*daily.* His words impart strength. God has hidden everything you are needing... *in His Word.* Daniel reveals the secret of his unstoppable power to be unmoved, "And when He had spoken unto me, I was strengthened," (Daniel 10:19).

Divine Energy Is Transferred Through Divine Words. Are you depressed? Read Psalm 37...or 91 aloud. It is astounding and startling to be instantly and immediately empowered. "The entrance of Thy Words giveth light," (Psalm 119:130).

Invest in my book entitled, *The 31 Greatest Chapters in The Bible.* Speak these sentences aloud now:

I *love* His Word.

I *live* by His Word.

I *speak* His Word.

I *listen* to His Word.

Study The Word of God. Every single day. You might start with one book at a time. Like Philemon, First Timothy or Ephesians. Take one book, read it that day. Just four, five or six chapters. Then, read it again the next day. Read it again the next day. Read it again the next day. And every day you read it, there will be something fresh and new for you. Study The Word. As Paul advised Timothy, "Study to shew thyself approved unto God," (2 Timothy 2:15).

There are at least three immediate rewards in studying the Bible.

1.   You Provide Proof Of Respect In The

Eyes Of God. When The Holy Spirit sees you sitting at His feet, He is authorized to become your Personal Mentor. Picture this: you are *reading* His Word, you are *thinking* on His Word, you are *studying* His Word.

    2.   You Attract Divine Favor *Immediately*.

    3.   Unexplainable Peace Enters.

Your Ritual of Honor silences any demonic attentiveness. It attracts angelic admiration.

You assess the worth of other people relative to their reaction to your words. Their reaction to your words reveals your importance to them. They may smile. They may wear expensive cologne. But their reaction to your words determines how you view them...Their value to you...Their future with you.

If you never read the Bible, it is a photograph of your dishonoring of it. Have a respect for God. Study The Word. Take your notes.

Remember, the first Ritual of Honor is *The Ritual Of Reading The Bible.*

RECOMMENDED INVESTMENTS:
31 Greatest Chapters in The Bible (Book/B-54/138 pages/$10)
The 3 Most Important Things In Your Life (Book/B-101/
  240 pages/$15)

Repetition
Births
Persuasion.

-MIKE MURDOCK

⤳ **2** ⤳

The Ritual Of Listening To The Word Of God

Listen Daily To The Word Of God On CD.
What Enters You Determines What Exits You.

What You *Hear* Determines What You *Feel.* "So, then faith cometh by hearing, and hearing by the word of God," (Romans 10:17). The immediate reward of listening...is Uncommon Faith.

Miracles that come to your life do not come because God loves you. They come because of your *faith in God.*

Your love for God does not produce Miracles.

The love of God for you does not produce Miracles.

Your Faith Decides Your Miracles.

Faith is confidence in God. *God's Only Pain Is To Be Doubted; God's Only Pleasure Is To Be Believed.*

What is the key to the 1,189 chapters of the Bible? "God is not a man, that He should lie; neither the son of man, that He should repent: hath He said, and shall He not do it? or hath He spoken, and shall He not make it good?" (Numbers 23:19).

Trust Is The Highest Proof Of Honor.

Relationships are Circles of need and influence

around your life. Every Circle is different in Need, Influence, Trust, Access and Benefits. I routinely analyze changes in relationships. Sometimes someone I have trusted becomes intimate with someone I distrust. That changes my Access Codes dramatically.

Wisdom Is The Study Of Difference.

Why is *listening*...a proven Ritual of Honor? It proves my passion for counsel...my confidence in Divine Wisdom...and humility demonstrated by my reaching. The greatest reward of listening to the Bible every day is that a passion for righteousness begins to grow... *immediately.*

My desire for righteousness begins as a Seed... that must be nourished and increased. Listening to the Bible is proof of Respect. It is the Factory for my Faith. *"Faith cometh by hearing, and hearing by The Word of God,"* (Romans 10:17).

Remember, the second Ritual of Honor is *The Ritual Of Listening To The Word Of God.*

RECOMMENDED INVESTMENTS:
31 Greatest Chapters in The Bible (Book/B-54/138 pages/$10)
The 3 Most Important Things In Your Life (Book/B-101/
  240 pages/$15)

⚍ 3 ⚎

THE RITUAL OF STUDYING WISDOM EVERY DAY

Wisdom Is The Master Key To Success.

The Scriptures teach this clearly that Wisdom should become the Priority Focus of every day of your life. "Wisdom is the principal thing," (Proverbs 4:7).

What is Wisdom? *Wisdom Is The Ability To Discern Difference.* There is a difference in people, moments, environments and opportunities. Solomon requested Wisdom and Understanding from God. God honored this wise request with Favor, Prosperity and Peace with adversaries.

Someone *knows* what you do not know.

Someone *sees* what you do not see.

Someone *has been* where you want to go.

What is the price you are willing to pay for the hidden treasure in them? You can gain a year of knowledge in 5 minutes...if you are willing to Ask, Seek, Knock. *The Proof Of Passion Is Pursuit.*

Questions host answers on the earth. Never seek for answers. They are the employees of Questions. A quality question is the greatest force on earth. Here are a few:

If I were my enemy, how would I destroy me?

What is my greatest passion, and what do I invest

daily in its pursuit?

Whose presence energizes me?

Who has recognized my Divine Assignment and honored it significantly?

What would I choose to do with my life, if money were not an issue?

If I could master any topic, what would it be?

What problems do I solve best?

What should I be doing to protect my Mind?

Your Mind is your greatest investment on earth. It is more important than your house, investment properties, stocks on Wall Street...even your family. Your Mind is the Garden where you grow the fruit that sustains you.

Your Mind...is where motivation begins. It is the Factory for your Energy, Creativity and Aura you exude in daily conversations.

That's why studying Wisdom must become a daily Ritual. God will honor it. It shows humility when you are able to learn from the writings and experiences of others.

Mistakes and Mentors are the two dominant sources of Wisdom.

- ▶ Decide what you want to know most about.
- ▶ Decide who knows more than you about it.
- ▶ Teach what you learn...as you are learning it.
- ▶ Be quick to ask questions freely.
- ▶ Admit what you do not know.

The Ritual of learning...is the greatest cure for depression, fear and passivity.

Remember, the third Ritual of Honor is *The Ritual Of Studying Wisdom Every Day.*

4

THE RITUAL OF CHURCH ATTENDANCE

Church Is A Life-Changing Experience.
Attending Church Is Also A Task.
Don't misunderstand me. I love the Presence of God. Hearing an audience worshipping and glorifying God is an experience beyond explanation. The environment of God's people is the closest thing to Heaven on earth. I love church. I love the Family of God. But...getting dressed, preparing, driving miles in the traffic is not a happy experience for me. So, I must remind myself that the sacrifice of preparation is a Seed God will honor.

Church attendance is obedience to a Divine Command. "Not forsaking the assembling of ourselves together, as the manner of some is; but exhorting one another: and so much the more, as ye see the day approaching," (Hebrews 10:25).

Uncommon leaders love the House of God. "I was glad when they said unto me, Let us go into the House of the Lord," (Psalm 122:1).

Church is where you discover the beauty of God and the solutions to your questions. "One thing have I desired of the Lord, that will I seek after; that I may dwell in the House of the Lord all the days of my life, to behold the beauty of the Lord, and to inquire in His temple," (Psalm 27:4).

Experiences occur in the sanctuary of worship that do not occur anywhere else. "And let them make Me a sanctuary; that I may dwell among them," (Exodus 25:8).

Jesus Had The Habit Of Going To The Synagogue. The Bible says, "as His custom was." "...as His custom was, He went into the synagogue on the sabbath day, and stood up for to read," (Luke 4:16).

I understand why some prefer the ease and convenience of staying home and watching Christian television.

That's why Church Attendance is such a *significant Ritual of Honor.*

Oh, the power of habit and custom!

The difference in men is in their habits. *Men Don't Decide Their Future; They Decide Their Habits And Their Habits Create Their Future.*

Your faithful attendance to the House of the Lord is a Ritual of Honor forever recorded in the heavenlies. Your love for the House of God guarantees the respect of God Himself toward you. Spiritual leaders are so strengthened and encouraged through those who show support to a man of God, communal impartation to each other, strengthening each other, encouraging each other.

Conversation.

Communion.

Commitment.

Comfort.

Church.

"Then they that feared the Lord spake often one to

another: and the Lord hearkened, and heard it, and a book of remembrance was written before Him for them that feared the Lord, and that thought upon His Name. And they shall be Mine, saith the Lord of hosts, in that day when I make up My jewels; and I will spare them, as a man spareth his own son that serveth him," (Malachi 3:16-17).

Oh, never waver from the Ritual of Honor... consistency in your faithfulness to attend the House of God!

Is it ceremonial? Yes.

Is it a ritual? Yes.

Do you sometimes feel weary of it? Yes.

Do you ever want to stay home? Of course.

That's what makes it a Ritual of true Honor.

Remember, the fourth Ritual of Honor is *The Ritual Of Church Attendance.*

Singing Is The Protocol
For Entering
The Spirit-World.

-MIKE MURDOCK

≈ 5 ≈

THE RITUAL OF SINGING AND WORSHIP

Singing Is A Command.

Singing is the protocol of the Spirit-world.

Read Psalm 100:1-2, 4-5: "Make a joyful noise unto the Lord, all ye lands. Serve the Lord with gladness: come before His presence with singing. Enter into His gates with thanksgiving, and into His courts with praise: be thankful unto Him, and bless His name. For the Lord is good."

Why? *For the Lord is good.*

Why the Ritual of Worship? Proof of Honor.

This Ritual of Worship is your invitation to The Holy Spirit. It guarantees a personal visitation from Him. Nothing impresses Him more.

You may think, "But Mike, I am not a singer!" I am not either. I have never viewed myself as a professional singer. I do not sing because I am a singer. I rarely listen to my own recordings though I am very thankful for the people who do. I sing because I am in love with The Holy Spirit. He is my very Life.

It was a secret of David, the sweet psalmist of Israel. When he played his harp in the courts of Saul, demon spirits departed. (See 1 Samuel 16:23).

Remember, the fifth Ritual of Honor is *The Ritual Of Singing And Worship.*

Environment Decides
What Lives Or Dies.

-MIKE MURDOCK

≈ 6 ≈

THE RITUAL OF THE SECRET PLACE

━━━▶▷-◦-◁◀━━━

Places Were Created Before People.

Places matter greatly. Where You Are Determines What Grows Within You—Your Weakness Or Your Strength.

Sanctify a place in your home where you will meet with The Holy Spirit each morning. You need a special place where you meet with the Lord...exclusively set apart for Him. Preferably a separate room. At least, invest in preparing a corner of the room, if nothing else is possible. "Sanctify yourselves, both ye and your brethren, that ye may bring up the ark of the Lord God of Israel unto the place that I have prepared for it," (1 Chronicles 15:12).

Where You Are Determines What Dies Inside You. Your doubts, your fears, your weaknesses. *Where You Are Determines What Thrives Within You.* Your faith, your confidence.

Schedule the first seven minutes of every day to enter His presence. Make it a Ritual of Honor. Sanctify a room at your house and make it a ritual. *The first seven minutes. What You Do First Determines What God Does Second.* The first seven minutes of every day. Remember, Seven is the number of completion. "The

Lord will perfect that which concerneth me," (Psalm 138:8).

Use your energy to *enter* His Presence. Let Him use His energy to *keep* you in His Presence. I highly recommend my book, *Where Miracles Are Born,* on establishing your prayer time each day.

10 Miracles That Happen In The Secret Place

1. It is the Room of *Hope*...where Impossibility Thinking becomes Possibility Thinking as you gaze upon the countenance of the One Who created you (Philippians 4:13).

2. It is the Room of *Love*...where the love of God is poured into you for others to receive from you (1 John 4:16).

3. It is the Room of *Change*...where hardened hearts become softened (Job 23:16).

4. It is the Room of *Forgiveness*...where every mistake you have made is removed (Psalm 103:12).

5. It is the Room of *Mercy*...where the guilt of sin is dissolved (Psalm 37:26).

6. It is the Room of *Decision-Making*...where accurate information is imparted, making quality decisions possible (Psalm 32:8).

7. It is the Room of *Financial Recovery*...where God's plan of survival becomes understood (Psalm 34:6).

8. It is the Room of *Wisdom*...where the Law of God is forever engraved on your heart (Proverbs 4:7).

9. It is the Room of *Waiting*...where the Seeds of Patience bear fruit (Isaiah 40:19-31).

10. It is the Room of *Joy*...where He rewards the obedient with the fragrance called Joy (Psalm 16:11).

Those who invest time in The Secret Place are rewarded with the secrets of God.

Remember, the sixth Ritual of Honor is *The Ritual Of The Secret Place.*

Tithing Creates
The Partnership
That Includes Protection.

-MIKE MURDOCK

7

THE RITUAL OF THE TITHE

The Tithe Is The First Ten Percent Of Your Income.
God describes it as holy. "And all the tithe of the land, whether of the seed of the land, or of the fruit of the tree, is the Lord's: it is holy unto the Lord. And concerning the tithe of the herd, or of the flock, even of whatsoever passeth under the rod, the tenth shall be holy unto the Lord," (Leviticus 27:30, 32).

Tithe is a Ritual of Honor. "Honour the Lord with thy substance, and with the firstfruits of all thine increase," (Proverbs 3:9).

Every Ritual of Honor schedules a guaranteed reward. "So shall thy barns be filled with plenty, and thy presses shall burst out with new wine," (Proverbs 3:10).

The Tithe means 10 percent of your income. The first dime of every dollar belongs to God. It is *His.* It is *Holy.* It is a *Ritual.* It is a *Ceremony.* But the Ritual of The Tithe guarantees financial favor. It guarantees that the covenant of partnership is at work.

Never forsake this Ritual of Presentation of The Tithe. The first thing we do every week in this ministry is to set aside The Tithe. Ten percent of everything that comes in—if I sell a book for $10.00, $1.00 goes for The Tithe. Tithe from the gross you receive, not the net.

Your Offering cannot begin until The Tithe has been returned...to the Lord.

Tithe is proof of Honor. It is proof of Obedience. And it silences the voices of 10,000 enemies. *Consistent Tithing* guarantees consistent reaping. If you are erratic in your *receiving* from God, this indicates that your obedience is probably inconsistent.

I really believe that you should covenant with The Holy Spirit through The Tithe. Tithe to the House of the Lord. Always Tithe wherever you are consistently receiving your spiritual food and teaching.

The Tithe always silences the devourer in your life.

The Tithe guarantees the Divine Favor of God.

Establish the Ritual of it. Do it *first.* Do not allow it to be a mind-trap. Make it a Heart-Covenant.

Remember, the seventh Ritual of Honor is *The Ritual Of The Tithe.*

Our Prayer Together...

"Holy Spirit, thank You for Your blessing, Your Presence and supernatural protection. I could not pay in money what I have received from You in Favor, good health and financial breakthrough. Today I make a covenant to Tithe for the rest of my life to Your great work. Everything I have came from You anyway... so I return The Tithe to You as a Ritual of Honor, wrapped with the Miracle of Expectation for an Uncommon Harvest. In the Name of Jesus, I call in my Harvest of 100-fold as You promised in Mark 10:28-30. It is done and I rejoice in my covenant partnership with You. In Jesus' Name, Amen."

DECISION

Will You Accept Jesus As Your Personal Savior Today?

The Bible says, "That if thou shalt confess with thy mouth the Lord Jesus, and shalt believe in thine heart that God hath raised Him from the dead, thou shalt be saved," (Romans 10:9).

Pray this prayer from your heart today!

"Dear Jesus, I believe that You died for me and rose again on the third day. I confess I am a sinner...I need Your love and forgiveness...Come into my heart. Forgive my sins. I receive Your eternal life. Confirm Your love by giving me peace, joy and supernatural love for others. Amen."

Clip and Mail

DR. MIKE MURDOCK

is in tremendous demand as one of the most dynamic speakers in America today.

More than 16,000 audiences in 40 countries have attended his Schools of Wisdom and conferences. Hundreds of invitations come to him from churches, colleges and business corporations. He is a noted author of over 200 books, including the best sellers, *The Leadership Secrets of Jesus* and *Secrets of the Richest Man Who Ever Lived.* Thousands view his weekly television program, *Wisdom Keys with Mike Murdock.* Many have attended his Schools of Wisdom that he hosts in major cities of America.

❑ Yes, Mike! I made a decision to accept Christ as my personal Savior today. Please send me my free gift of your book, *31 Keys to a New Beginning* to help me with my new life in Christ.

NAME _____ BIRTHDATE _____

ADDRESS _____

CITY _____ STATE _____ ZIP _____

PHONE _____ E-MAIL _____

Mail form to:
The Wisdom Center · 4051 Denton Hwy. · Ft. Worth, TX 76117
1-817-759-BOOK · 1-817-759-0300
You Will Love Our Website...! www.WisdomOnline.com

31

DR. MIKE MURDOCK

1 Has embraced his Assignment to Pursue...Proclaim...and Publish the Wisdom of God to help people achieve their dreams and goals.

2 Preached his first public sermon at the age of 8.

3 Preached his first evangelistic crusade at the age of 15.

4 Began full-time evangelism at the age of 19, which has continued since 1966.

5 Has traveled and spoken to more than 16,000 audiences in 40 countries, including East and West Africa, the Orient, Europe and South America.

6 Noted author of over 200 books, including best sellers, *Wisdom for Winning*, *Dream Seeds*, *The Double Diamond Principle*, *The Law of Recognition* and *The Holy Spirit Handbook*.

7 Created the popular *Topical Bible* series for Businessmen, Mothers, Fathers, Teenagers; *The One-Minute Pocket Bible* series, and *The Uncommon Life* series.

8 The Creator of The Master 7 Mentorship System, an Achievement Program for Believers.

9 Has composed thousands of songs such as "I Am Blessed," "You Can Make It," "God Rides On Wings Of Love" and "Jesus, Just The Mention Of Your Name," recorded by many gospel artists.

10 Is the Founder and Senior Pastor of The Wisdom Center in Fort Worth, Texas...a Church with International Ministry around the world.

11 Host of *Wisdom Keys with Mike Murdock,* a weekly TV Program seen internationally.

12 Has appeared often on TBN, CBN, BET, Daystar, Inspirational Network, LeSea Broadcasting and other television network programs.

13 Has led over 3,000 to accept the call into full-time ministry.

THE MINISTRY

1 **Wisdom Books & Literature** - Over 200 best-selling Wisdom Books and 70 Teaching Tape Series.

2 **Church Crusades** - Multitudes are ministered to in crusades and seminars throughout America in "The Uncommon Wisdom Conferences." Known as a man who loves pastors, he has focused on church crusades for over 41 years.

3 **Music Ministry** - Millions have been blessed by the anointed songwriting and singing of Mike Murdock, who has made over 15 music albums and CDs available.

4 **Television** - *Wisdom Keys with Mike Murdock,* a nationally-syndicated weekly television program.

5 **The Wisdom Center** - The Church and Ministry Offices where Dr. Murdock speaks weekly on Wisdom for The Uncommon Life.

6 **Schools of The Holy Spirit** - Mike Murdock hosts Schools of The Holy Spirit in many churches to mentor believers on the Person and Companionship of The Holy Spirit.

7 **Schools of Wisdom** - In many major cities Mike Murdock hosts Schools of Wisdom for those who want personalized and advanced training for achieving "The Uncommon Dream."

8 **Missions Outreach** - Dr. Mike Murdock's overseas outreaches to 40 countries have included crusades in East and West Africa, the Orient, Europe and South America.

Millionaire-Talk

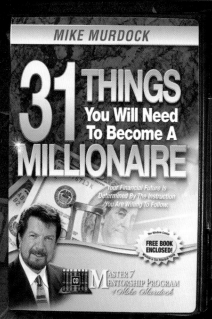

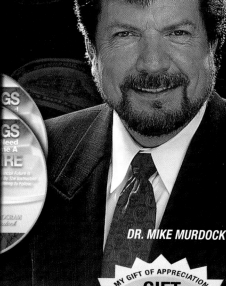

DR. MIKE MURDOCK

MY GIFT OF APPRECIATION
GIFT of Appreciation
Wisdom Is The Principal Thing

31 Things You Will Need To Become A Millionaire *(2-CD's/WCPL-116)*

Topics Include:

▷ *You Will Need Financial Heroes*
▷ *Your Willingness To Negotiate Everything*
▷ *You Must Have The Ability To Transfer Your Enthusiasm, Your Vision To Others*
▷ *Know Your Competition*
▷ *Be Willing To Train Your Team Personally As To Your Expectations*
▷ *Hire Professionals To Do A Professional's Job*

I have asked the Lord for 3,000 special partners who will sow an extra Seed of $58 towards our Television Outreach Ministry. Your Seed is so appreciated! Remember to request your Gift CD's, 2 Disc Volume, *31 Things You Will Need To Become A Millionaire,* when you write this week!

THE WISDOM CENTER
4051 Denton Highway • Fort Worth, TX 76117

1-817-759-BOOK
1-817-759-0300

You Will Love Our Website...!
www.WisdomOnline.com

A

Miracle 7
BOOK PAK!

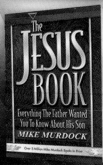

DR. MIKE MURDOCK

❶ **Dream Seeds** (Book/B-11/106pg/$9)

❷ **7 Hidden Keys to Favor** (Book/B-119/32pg/$7)

❸ **Seeds of Wisdom on Miracles** (Book/B-15/32pg/$3)

❹ **Seeds of Wisdom on Prayer** (Book/B-23/32pg/$3)

❺ **The Jesus Book** (Book/B-27/166pg/$10)

❻ **The Memory Bible on Miracles** (Book/B-208/32pg/$3)

❼ **The Mentor's Manna on Attitude** (Book/B-58/32pg/$3)

The Wisdom Center
Miracle 7 Book Pak!
Only **$30** $38 Value
Wisdom Is The Principal Thing
WBL-24

Add 10% For S/H

Quantity Prices Available Upon Request

Each Wisdom Book may be purchased separately if so desired.

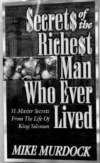

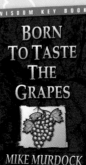

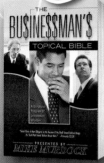 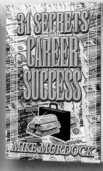  

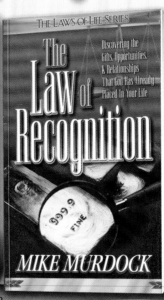

The
Businessman's Devotional 4
Book Pak!

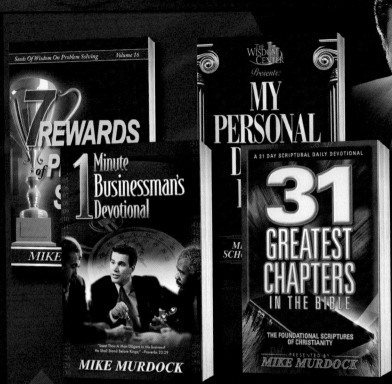

1 **7 Rewards of Problem-Solving** (Book/B-118/32pg/$7)

2 **My Personal Dream Book** (Book/B-143/32pg/$5)

3 **1 Minute Businessman's Devotional**
(Book/B-42/224pg/$12)

4 **31 Greatest Chapters In The Bible**
(Book/B-54/138pg/$10)

The Wisdom Center
**The
Businessman's
Devotional 4 Book Pak!**
Only $**20** $34 Value
PAK-22
Wisdom Is The Principal Thing

Add 10% For S/H

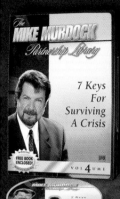

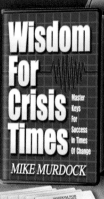

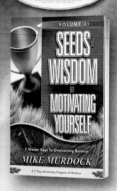
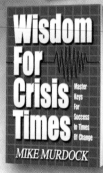

THE TURNAROUND Collection

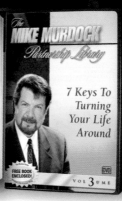
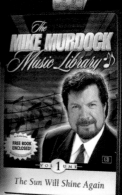

❶ The Wisdom Commentary Vol. 1 (Book/B-136/256pg/52 Topics/$25)

❷ Battle Techniques For War-Weary Saints (Book/B-07/32pg/$5)

❸ Seeds of Wisdom on Overcoming (Book/B-17/32pg/$3)

❹ The Memory Bible on Healing (Book/B-196/32pg/$3)

❺ How To Turn Your Mistakes Into Miracles (Book/B-56/32pg/$5)

❻ 7 Keys To Turning Your Life Around (DVD/MMPL-03D/$10)

❼ The Sun Will Shine Again (Music CD/MMML-01/$10)

Each Wisdom Product may be purchased separately if so desired.

The Wisdom Center
The Turnaround Collection
Only $40 $61 Value
PAK-15
Wisdom Is The Principal Thing

Add 10% For S/H

THE WISDOM CENTER
4051 Denton Highway • Fort Worth, TX 76117

1-817-759-BOOK
1-817-759-0300

You Will Love Our Website...!
www.WisdomOnline.com

Favor 4!

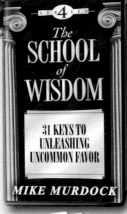 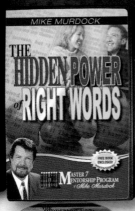 

This Collection Of Wisdom Will Change The Seasons Of Your Life Forever!

1. **The School of Wisdom #4 / 31 Keys To Unleashing Uncommon Favor...Tape Series** (6 Cassettes/TS-44/$30)

2. **The Hidden Power Of Right Words...** Master 7 Mentorship Program of Mike Murdock (CD/WCPL-27/$10)

3. **7 Hidden Keys to Favor** (Book/B-119/32pg/$7)

4. **Seeds of Wisdom on Obedience** (Book/B-20/32pg/$3)

Each Wisdom Product may be purchased separately if so desired.

The Wisdom Center
Favor 4 Collection!
Only $35 $50 Value
PAK-12
Wisdom Is The Principal Thing

Add 10% For S/H

J **THE WISDOM CENTER** 4051 Denton Highway • Fort Worth, TX 76117

1-817-759-BOOK
1-817-759-0300

You Will Love Our Website...!
www.WisdomOnline.com

Financial $ecrets.

THE 31 DAY MENTORSHIP PROGRAM
31 REASON$
PEOPLE DO NOT RECEIVE THEIR
FINANCIAL HARVE$T
MIKE MURDOCK

Buy One...
Receive The
Second One
FREE!
The Wisdom Center
Wisdom Is The Principal Thing

VIDEO
7 KEYS to 1000 TIMES MORE
The Lord God Of Your Fathers
Make You A Thousand Times
So Many More As You Are,
And Bless You, As He Hath
Promised You!
Deuteronomy 1:11
MIKE MURDOCK

VI-16

Your Financial World Will Change Forever.

Video 2-Pak!

▶ 8 Scriptural Reasons You Should Pursue Financial Prosperity

▶ The Secret Prayer Key You Need When Making A Financial Request To God

▶ The Weapon Of Expectation And The 5 Miracles It Unlocks

▶ How To Discern Those Who Qualify To Receive Your Financial Assistance

▶ How To Predict The Miracle Moment God Will Schedule Your Financial Breakthrough

▶ Habits Of Uncommon Achievers

▶ The Greatest Success Law I Ever Discovered

▶ How To Discern Your Place Of Assignment, The Only Place Financial Provision Is Guaranteed

▶ 3 Secret Keys In Solving Problems For Others

The Wisdom Center
Video 2-Pak!
Only **$30** $60 Value
VIPAK-01
Wisdom Is The Principal Thing

Add 10% For S/H

DISCOVER MasterCard VISA

Each Wisdom Product may be purchased separately if so desired.

THE WISDOM CENTER
4051 Denton Highway • Fort Worth, TX 76117

1-817-759-BOOK
1-817-759-0300

You Will Love Our Website...!
www.WisdomOnline.com

K

THE WISDOM BIBLE

Partnership Edition

Over 120 Wisdom Study Guides Included Such As:

- *10 Qualities Of Uncommon Achievers*
- *18 Facts You Should Know About The Anointing*
- *21 Facts To Help You Identify Those Assigned To You*
- *31 Facts You Should Know About Your Assignment*
- *8 Keys That Unlock Victory In Every Attack*
- *22 Defense Techniques To Remember During Seasons Of Personal Attack*
- *20 Wisdom Keys And Techniques To Remember During An Uncommon Battle*
- *11 Benefits You Can Expect From God*
- *31 Facts You Should Know About Favor*
- *The Covenant Of 58 Blessings*
- *7 Keys To Receiving Your Miracle*
- *16 Facts You Should Remember About Contentious People*
- *5 Facts Solomon Taught About Contracts*
- *7 Facts You Should Know About Conflict*
- *6 Steps That Can Unlock Your Self-Confidence*
- *And Much More!*

Your Partnership makes such a difference in The Wisdom Center Outreach Ministries. I wanted to place a Gift in your hand that could last a lifetime for you and your family...**The Wisdom Study Bible.**

40 Years of Personal Notes...this Partnership Edition Bible contains 160 pages of my Personal Study Notes...that could forever change your Bible Study of The Word of God. This **Partnership Edition...**is my personal **Gift of Appreciation** when you sow your Sponsorship Seed of $1,000 to help us complete The Prayer Center and TV Studio Complex. An Uncommon Seed Always Creates An Uncommon Harvest!

Mike

Thank you from my heart for your Seed of Obedience (Luke 6:38).

THE WISDOM CENTER
4051 Denton Highway • Fort Worth, TX 76117

1-817-759-BOOK
1-817-759-0300

You Will Love Our Website...!
www.WisdomOnline.com

L

This Gift Of Appreciation Will Change Your Bible Study For The Rest Of Your Life.

The Wisdom Bible

MY GIFT...
C
Your Sp
of $1
Praye
Stud
Wisdom Is

THE WISDOM CENTER
4051 Denton Highway • Fort Worth, TX 76117
1-817-759-BOOK
1-817-759-0300
You Will L.
www.Wis

Spirit Music.

The Mike Murdock Music Library

LOVE SONGS TO THE HOLY SPIRIT

Written In The Secret Place

TS-59

SERIES 1

...DOCK

LOVE SONGS TO THE HOLY SPIRIT

DR. MIKE MURDOCK

THE HOLY SPIRIT HANDBOOK

What You Need To Know About Your Daily Companion, The Holy Spirit

Volume

MI...

The Wisdom Center
Free Book ENCLOSED!
B-100 ($10 Value)
Wisdom Is The Principal Thing

Songs...

1. A Holy Place
2. Anything You Want
3. Everything Comes From You
4. Fill This Place With Your Presence
5. First Thing Every Morning
6. Holy Spirit, I Want To Hear You
7. Holy Spirit, Move Again
8. Holy Spirit, You Are Enough
9. I Don't Know What I Would Do Without You
10. I Let Go (Of Anything That Stops Me)
11. I'll Just Fall On You
12. I Love You, Holy Spirit
13. I'm Building My Life Around You
14. I'm Giving Myself To You
15. I'm In Love! I'm In Love!
16. I Need Water (Holy Spirit, You're My Well)
17. In The Secret Place

18. In Your Presence, I'm Always Changed
19. In Your Presence (Miracles Are Born)
20. I've Got To Live In Your Presence
21. I Want To Hear Your Voice
22. I Will Do Things Your Way
23. Just One Day At A Time
24. Meet Me In The Secret Place
25. More Than Ever Before
26. Nobody Else Does What You Do
27. No No Walls!
28. Nothing Else Matters Anymore (Since I've Been In The Presence Of You Lord)
29. Nowhere Else
30. Once Again You've Answered
31. Only A Fool Would Try (To Live Without You)
32. Take Me Now
33. Teach Me How To Please You

34. There's No Place I'd Rather Be
35. Thy Word Is All That Matters
36. When I Get In Your Presence
37. You're The Best Thing (That's Ever Happened To Me)
38. You Are Wonderful
39. You've Done It Once
40. You Keep Changing Me
41. You Satisfy

The Wisdom Center
6 Tapes/Only $30*
PAK007
Wisdom Is The Principal Thing

Add 10% For S/H

 N

THE WISDOM CENTER
4051 Denton Highway • Fort Worth, TX 76117

1-817-759-BOOK
1-817-759-0300

You Will Love Our Website...!
www.WisdomOnline.com